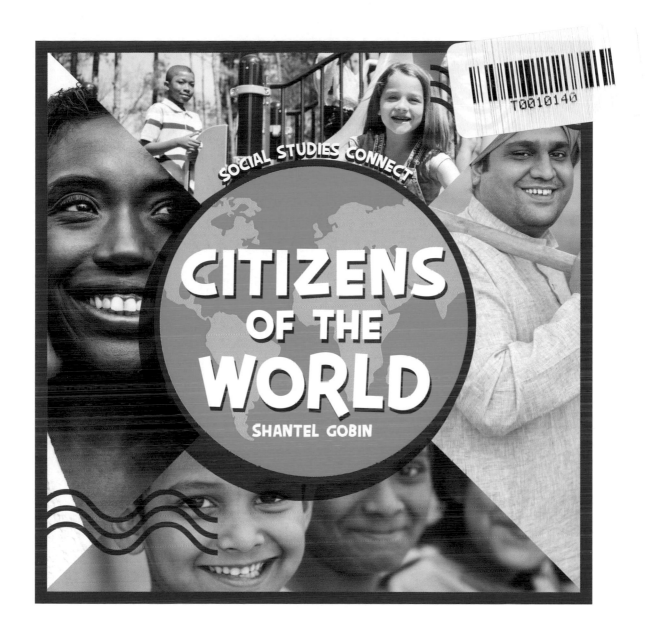

SOCIAL STUDIES CONNECT

CITIZENS
OF THE
WORLD

SHANTEL GOBIN

Rourke.

BEFORE AND DURING READING ACTIVITIES

Before Reading: *Building Background Knowledge and Vocabulary*

Building background knowledge can help children process new information and build upon what they already know. Before reading a book, it is important to tap into what children already know about the topic. This will help them develop their vocabulary and increase their reading comprehension.

Questions and Activities to Build Background Knowledge:

1. Look at the front cover of the book and read the title. What do you think this book will be about?
2. What do you already know about this topic?
3. Take a book walk and skim the pages. Look at the table of contents, photographs, captions, and bold words. Did these text features give you any information or predictions about what you will read in this book?

Vocabulary: *Vocabulary Is Key to Reading Comprehension*

Use the following directions to prompt a conversation about each word.

- Read the vocabulary words.
- What comes to mind when you see each word?
- What do you think each word means?

> ### Vocabulary Words:
>
> - *citizens*   - *cultures*
> - *continent*   - *laws*

During Reading: *Reading for Meaning and Understanding*

To achieve deep comprehension of a book, children are encouraged to use close reading strategies. During reading, it is important to have children stop and make connections. These connections result in deeper analysis and understanding of a book.

 Close Reading a Text

During reading, have children stop and talk about the following:

- Any confusing parts
- Any unknown words
- Text to text, text to self, text to world connections
- The main idea in each chapter or heading

Encourage children to use context clues to determine the meaning of any unknown words. These strategies will help children learn to analyze the text more thoroughly as they read.

When you are finished reading this book, turn to the last page for **After-Reading** activities.

TABLE OF CONTENTS

ONE WORLD

We live in many places.
We come from many **cultures**.

But we are one world!
We are **citizens** of the world.

WE LEARN

Children are everywhere.

Schools are everywhere.

IS YEAR-ROUND SCHOOL COOL?

In Japan, kids go to school all year. Do you think kids everywhere should go to school all year?

Around the world, kids learn in different spaces.

In Bangladesh and Brazil, some kids learn on boats. Welcome aboard!

WE LIVE

From California to Cambodia, some of us live in tiny houses.

DID YOU KNOW?

You can turn a school bus into a tiny house on wheels!

From England to Egypt, some of us live in skyscrapers!

WE WORK

Families farm all over the world, from Grenada to Greenland.

Potatoes for everybody!

FARMING JOBS ARE EVERYWHERE

Around the world, 40% of the population works in agriculture.

People work in offices on every **continent**. Some people make the **laws** of the land.

WE PLAY

On your mark. Get set. Go!
We run and play, even in Alaska.

DID YOU KNOW?

In Alaska, it can get colder than −70 degrees!

Goal! We play soccer. It is the most popular sport in the world.

SAME GAME, DIFFERENT NAME

Soccer is called "football" in most countries. Why do you think it is called that?

PHOTO GLOSSARY

citizens (SIT-i-zuhn-z): people who live in a particular town, city, country, or place

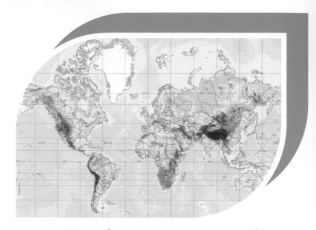

continent (KAHN-tuh-nuhnt): one of the seven large landmasses of the earth

cultures (KUHL-chur-z): the art, ideas, customs, traditions, and ways of life of groups of people

laws (law-z): rules that are established and enforced by a government